## CORONA, CORONA

Michael Hofmann was born in 1957 in Freiburg, Germany, and came to England in 1961. He was for seven years a student at Cambridge, and since 1983 has lived in London.

As well as two previous books of poems, he has published a number of translations from the German and his version of Brecht's *The Good Person of Sichuan* was performed at the National Theatre in London. He is at present editing an anthology on the theme of exile for Faber and Faber, and, with James Lasdun, a collection of translations by contemporary poets from Ovid's *Metamorphoses*.

# CORONA, CORONA

## Michael Hofmann

*faber and faber*

LONDON · BOSTON

First published in 1993
by Faber and Faber Limited
3 Queen Square London WC1N 3AU

Phototypeset by Wilmaset Ltd, Wirral
Printed by Clays Ltd, St Ives plc

A CIP record for this book is available from the British Library

ISBN 0–571–16962–7
      0–571–17052–8 (pbk)

10 9 8 7 6 5 4 3 2 1

for my kids

# Acknowledgements and Thanks

*Antaeus, Art International, Columbia, Honest Ulsterman,*
*London Review of Books, New Statesman and Society,*
*New Writing II* (Minerva), *Partisan Review,*
*PBS Anthologies* of 1988 and 1992 (Hutchinson),
*PEN New Poetry II* (Quartet), *PN Review, Poetry Ireland*
*Review, Quarry, Soho Square I* (Bloomsbury), *Thames Poetry*
(1990), *Times Literary Supplement, Voices.*

'Shivery Stomp' first appeared in *Malcolm Lowry Eighty Years*
*On*, edited by Sue Vice (Macmillan).

'A Minute's Silence' and 'On the Beach at Thorpeness' won the
*New Statesman*'s Prudence Farmer Prize in 1986 and 1988.

I would like to thank the Harper-Wood Foundation and St
John's College, Cambridge, for a studentship that made it
possible for me to spend some of 1988 and 1989 in Mexico.

M.H.

# Contents

I

# Lament for Crassus

Who grows old in fifty pages of Plutarch:
mores, omens, campaigns, Marius at sixty,
fighting fit, working out on the Campus Martius?

It surely isn't me, pushing thirty, taking a life a night,
my head on a bookshelf, five shelves of books overhead,
the bed either a classic or remaindered?

– I read about Crassus, who owned most of Rome.
Crassus, the third man, the third triumvir,
the second term in any calculation.

Crassus, the pioneer of insuranburn,
with his architect slaves and firefighter slaves,
big in silver, big in real estate, big in personnel.

Crassus, who had his name linked with a Vestal Virgin,
but was only after her house in the suburbs.
Crassus of bread and suburbs and circuses,

made Consul for his circuses, Crassus
*impresario*, not Crassus *imperator*, Crassus
who tried to break the military-political nexus.

Crassus, the inventor of the demi-pension holiday,
holed up in a cave on the coast of Spain for a month,
getting his dinner put out for him, and a couple of slave-girls.

Crassus, whose standards wouldn't rise on the final day,
who came out of his corner in careless black,
whose head was severed a day later than his son's.

# Biology

The brick ship of Victorian science
steamed on, ivy beard, iron beams and stairs,

iron paddleboat pillars. A pair of whiskery Germans,
father and son, had specialized in fixing in glass

some of the degenerative conditions of fruit.
A split blue peach, a bough laden with gangrene –

all pocked, opaque, Venetian, venereal . . .
Dry air, manila light, cardboard and silence,

anything to stave off the time when the exhibits
will revert to parrot dyes, wire and sand.

# The Late Richard Dadd, 1817–1886

The *Kentish Independent* of 1843
carried his pictures of his father, himself
and the scene of his crime. The first photo-journalist:
fairy-painter, father-slayer, poor, bad, mad Richard Dadd.

His extended Grand Tour took in the Holy Land
and ended in Bethlem Hospital, with its long panoptical
galleries, spider-plants, whippets and double-gaslights.
He had outlived himself at twenty-six . . .

There was one day he seemed to catch sunstroke.
He fancied the black, scorched beard of a sheik
would furnish him with some 'capital paintbrushes'.
Sailing up the Nile, on the *Hecate*,

they spent Christmas Day eating boiled eggs
and plum pudding, and playing cards for the captain's soul.
The temples at Luxor stood under a full moon, lightly boiled.
Sir Thomas got off to try and bag a crocodile.

The route up from Marseille went as the crow flies –
precipitately, a dash from ear to ear.
A fellow-traveller let him play with his collar and tie,
until he pulled out 'an excellent English razor'.

There was his watercolour, 'Dead Camel',
and a series of drawings of his friends,
all with their throats cut,
Frith, Egg, Dadd, Phillip and O'Neill.

He saw himself as a catspaw, Osiris's right-hand man
on earth. His digs in Newman Street
contained three hundred eggs, and the earth
cracked when he walked on it.

# Max Beckmann: 1915

Nurse, aesthetician and war-artist:
not unpatriotic, not unfeeling.
Calm – excitable. Noted yellow shell-holes,
the pink bones of a village steeple, a heated purple sky.
Bombardments. Tricks of the light. Graphic wounds.

An aviator overflew him in the rose night,
buzzed him, performed for him. Friend or foe? *Libellule*!
A room of his own in a villa. *Kriegsblick*.
Medics intellectually stimulating,
one, from Hamburg, familiar with his work.

A commission to decorate the baths
– an Oriental scene, how asinine! –
deserts, palmettoes, oases, dead Anzacs, Dardanelles.
A second fresco, of the bathhouse personnel.
One thousand male nudes per diem.

A prey to faces. Went for a squinting Cranach.
A man with half a head laughed at his sketches,
recognizing his companions. ('He died today.')
'Several hours' tigerish combat, then gave up
the assault': his description of a sitting.

Some *esprit de corps*. Marching songs
weirdly soothing, took him out of himself.
Ha, the amusing pretensions of a civilian
trying to commandeer a hotel room.
English prisoners, thirsty mudlarks, plucky, droll.

In the trenches the men had kissed their lives goodbye.
A ricochet, a sniper. In the midst of life.
Crosses plugging foxholes, stabbed into sandbags.
A man with a pistol, head down, intent, hunting rats.
Another, frying spuds on a buddy's grave.

The Flemish clocks told German time.
*Sekt* and Mosel to wash down the yellow *vin de pays*.
Dr Bonenfant, with his boozy babyface.
'We poor children.' A commission
to illustrate the army songbook. Invalided out.

# Ska

The man in Bermudas
with a chemo-Mohican
hip-limps into the sea,
is seen hopping still
between the feeble waves.

# Hart Crane

The territorial integrity of a battlefield:
a small state without frontiers, guarantors or governance,
without its own flag to run up its own flagpole
– an arm waving in the Caribbean, drowning –
a power vacuum ringed by lifeboats.

His name hardly fit a natural human man,
more an amalgamation, the merger of parent companies:
one surname after another, mother's, father's,
his sugar daddy, Peppermint Candy Cane Crane.
'In all the world no sweets like these.'

Dada, boom and Prohibition pushed him
the way of symbolism, Spengler, fruit-and-flower wines.
A sufficiency of drink, the manic repetition
of a mantric record – any record – and he typed.
Corona, Corona, Victrola and a Columbia loud needle.

Hollywood fellatio, the 'ancient mariner' dragging
Sands Street for sailors, standing on Brooklyn Bridge
with the US Navy steaming between his legs.
Stout Hart Crane with his sweet embonpoint,
a pud of pulchritude, lustre to his cluster.

Cigar eyes, shellac eyes, chocolate spaniel eyes.
Shoulder to shoulder with his father in Chagrin Falls,
cigars, canes, plod shoes, a twin squeezed benignity
in fat black double-breasted coats. He took up the hem
of his father's tombstone with his landless name.

# Kurt Schwitters in Lakeland

'Like nothing else in Tennessee' – Wallace Stevens


It was between greens (bowling, cricket),
but the graveyard had stayed immune, half-cut, and smelling
the yellow, abandoned smell of hay. A couple were casting
dead flowers into a wire trash-coop.

Kurt Schwitters's tombstone was hewn in straight lines,
*klipp und klar*, in the shape of a hat, brim – crown.
Unseasonable, but undeniably local,
someone had left a dozen daffodils.

The man had flown: a refugee,
then interned on the Isle of Man;
released, dead, exhumed, and returned to Germany,
to vote with his feet for the 1950s.

\*

His *Merz* was nothing to do with pain or March:
it had been withdrawn from the *Kommerz- und Privatbank*.
Each day he caught the early bus to work,
climbed up to his barn through a jungle of rhododendrons,

and built on to his *Merzwall*. – It too was moved,
cased in a steel frame, and keelhauled down the hill.
The one thing still there that his hands had touched
was a stone on the sill

of the picture window that had been put in
in place of the wall. It had an air
of having been given a spin,
a duck, a drakkar, a curling-stone.

# '50s Cuba

It was the farcical fast fast slow world
of dancing, miscegenation and cigars.
Africanized Neoclassical New Spain,
where Hannibal was brother to Caesar.
The dawn coup gave promise of a *mañana esplendorosa*.

Havana was Latin Vegas, Cadillac City.
Aid, investment and tourism were all up.
The prostitutes walked out on Virtue Street.
The U.S. Ambassador was the man to know.
American industrialists picked up awards.

Batista was Presley with canasta and phone taps and horror
                                                        movies.
He sat up in his off-limits audio-visual eyrie
with the lift hooked up like a rope ladder,
reading *The Day Lincoln was Shot*, while downstairs
his bodyguards wiped the floor with insurgents.

The jumpy radio told the time once a minute.
The rebels ran rings round an American reporter:
they each got nine innings, like a cat
or a baseball team. Cane plantations were
set alight by revolutionary Molotov rats . . .

The Ortodoxos dissolved, and jewelled ladies,
panicking for the exit, found only sugar-frosted mirrors
where they scratched their names.
Camilo Cienfuegos was lost at sea like Glenn Milller.
Asylants sifted round an archipelago of embassies.

# Salad

The salad man
            working six dollars an hour
                        nights
fisherman
            frequenter of prostitutes
                        paroled killer
boasting
            over in the night bakery
                        mystery trips
some catch
            Miss Trippi
                        down on the Genesee River
when the police found him
            parked on the bridge
                        the white parka
alone in his car
            sitting eating a salad
                        the body
Miss Cicero
            troubling
                        the creek below.

# Marvin Gaye

He added the final 'e'
to counteract the imputation of homosexuality.
His father was plain Revd Gay, his son Marvin III.

He slept with his first hooker
in the army, coming off saltpetre.
He thought there was another word for 'virgin' that wasn't
                                                    'eunuch'.

Including duets, he had fifty-five chart entries.
His life followed the rhythm of albums and tours.
He had a 'couple of periods of longevity with a woman'.

He preached sex to the cream suits,
the halter tops and the drug-induced personality disorders.
When his hair receded, he grew a woolly hat and beard.

Success was the mother of eccentricity and withdrawal.
In Ostend he felt the eyes of the Belgians on him,
in Topanga someone cut the throats of his two Great Danes.

At forty-four, back in his parents' house,
any one of a number of Marvins might come downstairs.
A dog collar shot a purple dressing-gown, twice.

**II**

# Sally

A blue button-through day, a pink, a black,
the little black dress, the bricks circulating
painfully through the central heating system,
sorrow, lust and peristalsis at three.

# Freebird

'One forms not the faintest inward attachment, especially here
   in America.' – D. H. Lawrence


Six girls round the pool in Stranglers' weather,
tanning; then three; then one (my favourite!),
every so often misting herself
or taking a drink of ice water from a plastic beaker.

Only the pool shark ever swam,
humming, vacuuming debris, cleverly avoiding its tail.
The white undersides of the mockingbirds
flashed green when they flew over.

The setting was a blue by pink downtown development,
Southern hurricane architecture in matchwood:
live-oaks and love-seats, handymen and squirrels,
an electric grille and a siege mentality.

The soil was cedar chips, sprinkler heads and ants.
A few transplanted azaleas with difficulty flowered.
On watering days,
the air stank of artesian sulphur.

I was cuntstruck and fat. My tight chinos
came from a Second Avenue surplus store
that had an RPG dangling from the ceiling.
Grenada had been; the campus killings came later.

I lived in three bare rooms and a walk-in refrigerator.
The telephone kept ringing for Furniture World.
I looked at the dirty waves
breaking on the blue carpet and said not exactly.

A con-artist called Washington showed me Greek letters
carved in his huge upper arm, and the pest control man,
his cry of a soul in pain, switched
the clicking roach boxes under the sink.

The frat boy overhead gave it to his sorority girl
                                    steamhammer-style.
Someone turned up the Lynyrd Skynyrd,
the number with the seven-minute instrumental coda.
Her little screams petered out, *inachevée*.

# Up in the Air

The sky was breaking, and I felt little less numb
than the alcoholic devotedly spooning
pâté from a tub; than the divorcee's station wagon
with its dog-haired sheepskin dogseat;
or the birds barking in the trees to greet the day . . .

There was a grey heron standing on a green bank.
'Soul survivors' spilled out of the *Titanic*
in their once-fluorescent sailing whites.
You only live once. The record sang 'My Girl',
but that was a lie. She only shucked my cigarette packet,

as she danced before my eyes like the alphabet,
mostly like the letter A . . . I was Ajax,
I had stolen another man's captive, slaughtered sheep
like a maniac, counted my friends till
I fell asleep, now I would have to swim for it

in the greasy, yellow, woollen waves . . .
The bass drum went like a heart, there was a pillow
curled in the bottom of it for anchorage.
Our finger-joints shook in the free air,
sheep's knuckle-bones dicing for the seamless garment.

Three hours flat out on the hotel candlewick,
blunting my creases, then off to the airport
with its complement of tiny, specialized, ministering
vehicles. I sat over the wing, rivetted, wary,
remembering ring fingers and flying kites.

# Wheels

Even the piss-artist, rocking back and forth
on the balls of his feet like a musical policeman,
is making an irreversible commitment . . . He shivers.

(The faith, application and know-how it takes
to do anything, even under controlled circumstances!)
I find in myself this absurd purposefulness;

walking through my house, I lean forward,
I lick my finger to open a door, to turn over a page,
or the page of a calendar, or an advent calendar.

It takes all day to read twenty pages,
and the day goes down in a blaze of television.
One blue day is much like another . . . The plane lands

with a mew of rubber and a few 'less-than' signs.
The ball, remembering who hit it, keeps going.
The choreographed car-chase is ruinously exciting,

but the wheels turn very slowly backwards,
to convince the viewer that, far from wasting time,
he's recreating himself. A Christmas Special!

From the great outdoors, there's the derision
of real cars, the honeyed drone of approachable taxis,
some man's immortal Jag, numbered DEB1T . . .

How it must cut past the huddle of water-blue Inyacars,
lining the elbow of the road: smashed imperatives,
wheelchair hulls, rhombuses, stalled quartz.

# Schönlaternengasse

Better never than late like the modern concrete
firetrap firegaps spacing the Austrian baroque, *risi pisi*;
like the morgenstern lamp's flex leaking plastic links of gold,
leaving the cutglass nightlight good enough to drink;
like the same tulip reproduction twice in our hapless room,
where the twelve lines of a spider plant die without offshoot:
your period, which we both half-hoped wouldn't come.

# Dean Point

It was some kind of quarry, a great excavation –
caterpillar treads, surface water, lumps of clay,
the mess of possibilities . . . It bore the forbidden,
almost criminal aspect of industrial premises.

Ramps led down from one level circle to another,
three or four turns of a gigantic blunt screw.
Corrugated iron towers passed among themselves
on conveyor belts whatever was produced there,

and there was a blue-water harbour where it might be
transported along the coast, or to another coast.
We couldn't have told it from by-product or waste.
The soft rock fell to pieces in my hands.

To one side was a beach, with stones and trash.
Spongy sea-plants grew on it, and what looked like
bloodied thigh-bones but were only a different seaweed.
The sea spilt itself a little way on to the grey sand.

# The Day After

I arrived on a warm day, early, a Sunday.
They were sweeping the gravel dunts of boules,
clearing away the wire rig and char of fireworks.
The red metal ornamental maples, planed and spinning
like globes on stalks, had caught the sun.

The cups of the fountains were running over.
A few drops rolled back on the underside, trailed along,
tense and brimming, and fell into the common pool
like ships going over the edge of the world:
the roaring waters, the stolid, day-long rainbow . . .

It struck eight, nine. There was no wind
to blow the glassy fountains off course. My eyes hurt
from the silver bedding plants and vermilion flowers.
I could almost believe the smooth, slabbed plinth
that said: They will rise again.

# From A to B and Back Again

The Northern Line had come out into the open,
was leaving tracks like a curving cicatrice.
There was Barnet, my glottal stop, trying hard
to live up to its name, colloquial and harmless and trite.

The place was sunny and congested, brick and green trim,
it had the one-of-everything-and-two-butchers
of a provincial town. First, I dropped into
the maternity hospital by accident . . .

The porter was an analphabete, but together
we found your name, down among the Os,
and there you were, my brave love,
in a loose hospital gown that covered nothing;

pale; on an empty drip; and eager to show me
your scars, a couple of tidy crosses
like grappling hooks, one in the metropolis,
the other some distance away, in the unconcerned suburbs.

# A Minute's Silence

*i.m. Michael Heffernan*

A seagull murmur or worse – he kept it quiet,
went at his work, made plans. One of his last,
he produced Hugo von Hofmannsthal's fictional
abdication, the Lord Chandos Letter, for radio:
a droll package of Ms and Hs and Fs and Ns –

his, and Hofmannsthal's, and mine, the translator's . . .
The studio was round the corner from Broadcasting House,
in a shakier, worse-favoured building,
hollowed under by the Piccadilly and Victoria Lines
drumming through Regent Street. One minute in three

was useless, a minute's silence, to avoid picking up
the awful judder at the heart of the city . . .
A year on, I'm in a new house and he's dead.
Traffic noises, clean slates hammered down –
to hear the banging, you wouldn't give them a price.

I'm sitting coiled over my letter of condolence,
head down, left elbow out, the verbs tramping stiffly
into the furthest corners of mood and tense, closed
conditionals, Latin and peculiar pluperfects,
like Hofmannsthal's . . . 'I had had no idea . . .'

# Avenue A

*for Pia and James*


The left leg of the sparrow was dead straight, turned out
    and useless,
like a ski facing backwards. He hopped about on the feeder
    on his good leg,
twittered and fluttered, curtseyed at the feed hatch. Two
    newcomers sidled up,
drove him along the window ledge, dipped their beaks into
    his mealy throat and fed.

# Retrospect

Back in 1961, the police had nothing more on their plates
than whose was the bicycle on the pavement
constituting a possible hazard?
I might have prayed for Sunday

never to come, the interview with a constable
paying a house-call, a helmet to stun the ceiling,
the mesmeric ER on the badge:
the *Fremdenpolizei* come to repatriate me.

I still worshipped a blue acute Anglia
for the name and the brainy space in the back,
a cerebellum like Richard Ellingham's. *Si pacem vis* . . .
The bicycle went to the lowest bidder.

                              *

I remembered only the declivity
of St Andrew's Hill when I saw it again,
not the gloomy elderberry ravening in front of the house,
not even the address on Windsor Road,

an Edwardian nest of damp and peckish students,
only the slope of the road – into nothing,
into a Severn-inspired silver, a scintilla . . .
As I climbed the street again, with the carpetbagging

eyes of a yapping estate-agent, a Cedric or a Damon,
there was a blind man coming the other way,
so very much at home there, he stopped at the gate
to crumble his white stick into his pocket.

# 47° Latitude

I was lying out on the caesium lawn,
on the ribs and ligatures of a split deckchair,
under the Roman purple of a copper beech,
a misgrown fasces, all rods and no axe.

It was the double-zero summer, where the birds
stunned themselves on the picture windows
with no red bird cardboard cut-out doubles to warn them,
where the puffball dandelion grew twice as high,

where it was better not to eat parsley.
Every Friday, the newspapers gave fresh readings,
and put Turkish hazelnuts on the index.
A becquerel might be a fish or a type of mushroom.

In Munich, cylindrical missile balloons
bounced table-high, head-high, caber-high, house-high.
The crowds on the Leopoldstrasse were thick as pebbles
on the beach. I lay out on the caesium lawn.

# Pastorale

*for Beat Sterchi*

Where the cars razored past on the blue highway,
I walked, unreasonably, *contre-sens*,

the slewed census-taker on the green verge,
noting a hedgehog's defensive needle-spill,

the bullet-copper and bullet-steel of pheasants,
henna ferns and a six-pack of Feminax,

indecipherable cans and the cursive snout and tail
of a flattened rat under the floribund ivy,

the farmer's stockpiled hayrolls and his flocks,
ancillary, bacillary blocks of anthrax.

# On the Beach at Thorpeness

I looked idly right for corpses in the underbrush,
then left, to check that Sizewell was still there.
The wind was from that quarter, northeasterly, a seawind,
B-wind, from that triune reliable fissile block.

– It blackened the drainage ditches
on the low coastal plain, blew up a dry tushing rustle
from the liberal-democratic Aesopian bullrushes,
and an ill-tempered creaking from Christian oaks . . .

A set of three-point lion prints padded up the beach.
The tideline was a ravel of seaweed and detritus,
a red ragged square of John Bull plastic,
a gull's feather lying down by a fishspine.

The North Sea was a yeasty, sudsy brown slop.
My feet jingled on the sloping gravel,
a crisp musical shingle. My tracks were oval holes
like whole notes or snowshoes or Dover soles.

Roaring waves of fighters headed back to Bentwaters.
The tide advanced in blunt codshead curves,
ebbed through the chattering teeth of the pebbles.
Jaw jaw. War war.

# Shivery Stomp

To see the trees spilled, the sap stanched with sawdust,
the ground flap open like a grave. The crippled raven,
conductor of souls, squatting by on a concrete pile,
cawing. The daytime moon (naturally) gibbous.

It produces a strange adjacency,
to have visited so many of your sites, Ripe and Rye,
Cuernavaca and Cambridge, and, by fifty-nine days,
never to have done time – a term – together.

Late Lowry in towelling shirt, rucksack and duck pants.
Thirty years late Lowry. Thirty years to name the jazzer's
                                        beard,
and the talents, forever falling short of professions,
like the naming of jazz numbers and combos.

The having usurped you thirty years –
down to sitting in an overwindowed 1940s lounge,
the mousy seaside furniture, the natural gas, the Home Service,
the long fourteenth, the links course, the South Coast.

The whole town turned out by the same brickworks,
one tailor and one sunset bolt of cloth.
Brick and lichen, pruned willow, prunes and the WI.
The England you fled and died in.

The bodiless wren, a tail and a teaspoon,
dipping down the street of cottage hospitals.
The Pied Piper fried food van
belting out 'Greensleeves' in a poor estate.

The gulls, floating and gorging on the coley-coloured water.
The hunkering on the rocks in my herringbone coat,
watching the fishermen swing their boats round
and point them back down the beach, ready for Tuesday.

The field, so comprehensively settled with starlings,
the farmer might have sown them there, starling
seeds, something perhaps like the frozen dew
I chip ahead of me in the light rough.

**III**

# Postcard from Cuernavaca

*to Ralph Manheim*


Picture me
sitting between the flying buttresses of Cuernavaca Cathedral
reading Lawrence on the clitoral orgasm, and (more!)
his notion of replacing the Virgin Mary,
the one enduringly popular foreigner,
with Cortez' translator, later mistress, la Malinche,
the one enduringly unpopular—because xenophile—Mexican...

The night wind
blows the clouds over from the direction of his old palace,
a rather gloomy, conglomerate affair, pirated from an old
                                        pyramid,
and studded with red volcanic tufa in heart-sized pieces.
It's an even-handed museum now: offensively large statue of
                                        Cortez —
revisionist Rivera mural. (Or you turn away from both,
and look to where the volcanoes used to be.)

Out in front,
there are forests of helium balloons glittering under the fresno
                                        trees
where sociable black grackles natter and scream.
Hawkers trailing by in profile like matadors, trailing – in one
                                        case a hawk.
A Mariachi trumpeter, wearing just his old pesos,
trilling drily into the gutter. Ostensible Aztecs
stitching their silver Roman-style tunics *im Schneidersitz*.

There's a band
hidden in Eiffel's unilluminated iron snowdrop bandstand –
bought by the Austrians here to cheer them up
when Maximilian left the scene – giving it some humpity.
The rondure and Prussian gleam of the horns –
I sit and listen in the Café Viena.
Anything north of here goes, and most things east.

My room is both.
A steel door, pasteboard panelling,
and so high it makes me dizzy.
The toilet paper dangles inquiringly from the window cross.
A light bulb's skull tumbles forlornly into the room.
Outside there is a chained monkey who bites. He lives,
as I do, on Coke and bananas, which he doesn't trouble to peel.

# Las Casas

I leaned round the corner in a Gold Rush town –
fortunate, apprehensive and somewhat surprised to be there.
The wind was one hazard, and so were the ramps
and unevennesses on the pavements, and the streetsellers
with their *montóns* of oranges. The kerbs were high,
almost a foot, as though anticipating a flood or blizzard.
Everyone seemed to have come from somewhere else,
the gringos from Europe and North America, the Ladinos,
once, ditto, the Indians from their outlying villages.
Everyone was a source of money to everyone else.
Who had it: the pink- or blue-burned and -burnoused
Indians; the women, in their bosoms with their babies;
the kerchiefed figures bussed in on the back of *camións*;
the ugly, leggy, insouciant foreign girls;
or the Ladinos, of whom the Indians said
they were begotten by a Ladina and a dog
by the side of the road, 'the Ladina helping' . . . ?
It was a raw town. The shoe shops sold mincing machines,
hats and aluminium buckets shared a shelf, paper and iron
went together – for the staking of claims, perhaps?
A town of radio shops and funeral parlours –
the dead travelled to the aquamarine graveyard
in station wagons, horizontal, to music;
the living, upright, on pickups, also to music.
Of well-lit drink shops. Of illustrated marriage magazines
and spot-the-beachball shots in Kodak shops.
Of *Secrets of a Nunnery*, and two churches
facing each other on two hills, holding a lofty dialogue.
(One was a ruin.) Of patio-and-parapet housing,
and pastel shacks whose quick spread swallowed the airport.

Of unpaved streets, away from the centre.
Of everyone off the streets, paved or not, by eight o'clock.
Of the all-day screech of tortilla machines
and the scrape of rockets up the sky, a flash in the pan,
a percussive crash, a surprisingly durable cloud.
Jubilation, and no eyes raised.

# Dégringolade

*for Hugo Williams*


The broken hydraulics squealing, or the mean
fiddler on the cowpunk cassette, or a needle
mauling the worn brake block on twisty Route 1
in white earth country by the Selegua River
on the San Andreas Fault: cliffs crowding the road,
trees handing each other down between the cliffs,
Spanish moss cascading down the trees.

# Calle 12 Septiembre

The street girl,
    the baby octopus,
        the helicopter
whirling overhead
    in the disturbance,
        in the uprising,
dipping, dripping light . . .
    The red sauce
        on the walls,
the plainclothes cars
    reversing at speed,
        white handkerchiefs out,
the foreign banks
    a busted flush,
        and 2000 ptes light
of *une pipe*
    and *l'amour*
        with 'Conchita'.

# The Out-of-Power

I walked on New Year's Eve from Trotsky's house
under the lindens, banana and rubber trees
of the Calle Viena – the jerried watchtowers,
the outside windows all bricked up or half-bricked in,
and the place where the crazed muralist Siqueiros
had sprayed the walls with automatic fire and still missed –

to the house of ex-President de la Madrid,
just two weeks out of office, and a reduced
ex-presidential complement of three guards on the pavement –
a glimpse down the drive to parked imported cars,
the pool, flowering shrubs, *frou-frou*, rhubarb,
glass in the windows, ice clinking in the glasses.

# One Man's Mexico

The forty-first country to introduce
hair-extension treatment.

# Progreso

The crazy zocalo tips at a loco angle.
It pours three hundred infant girls, dressed
like Christmas-tree fairies, down the church's throat, singing.
A thin trickle of demonstrators chant 'Mexico!' uphill.

Whitewashed against white ants, the yew tree trunks
look spindly and phosphorescent, like stalagmites
in the cavern of their shade. The birds won't sing.
An old man clutches a fistful of drumsticks and shivers.

A month after the election, the posters are still up,
each x-ing out counted as a vote for the winner,
the loser has lost his shirt and scowls like a prizefighter,
and the Party of the Institutionalized Revolution marches on.

Every shoe is a spurred boot, every hat is a stetson,
every car a Dodge pickup. In hat and boots, every man is
                                        seven feet tall,
twelve standing on his Dodge. On Coffinmaker Street,
a bottle goes from hand to hand, from the left hand to the
                                        right.

## 'No Company but Fear'

I eat alone in a room with a net
hanging from the ceiling; a red room, Roman red,
boss-eyed with pots, wall-eyed with pots,
a cracked gleam coming from the eyes of cracked pots,
giving my table talk to two parrots.

# Sunday in Puebla

*dies amara valde*

I saw the same face
on the bloody Jerusalem Christ in Puebla Cathedral,
on the 'Martyr of the Revolution', Aquiles Serdan,
and the law student, Gumaro Amaro Ramirez.

The Christ lay coffined in glass like Lenin.
He had more than the usual five wounds,
he had all the abrasions and contusions consistent with being
                                                    crucified.
– He must have been the work of a police artist.

In 1910, the police laid siege to Serdan's house
(now the Original Museum of the Mexican Revolution).
It was a slow night,
he hid under the floorboards for eighteen hours –

there was the neat trapdoor, out of *Doctor Faustus* or *Don
                                                Giovanni* –
and when he came up, crying 'Don't shoot!'
one bullet passed through his windpipe,
another unhinged the top of his head.

Gumaro had his life-sized picture
in a colour tabloid,
though his skin was white, and his blood almost black.
It was said the Governor had wanted him dead.

A dreadful indifference took me
in the room full of Mexican tricolors –
the same eagle on the same cactus chewing on the same
                                    worm –
and in the room of mildly heretical old banknotes,

the room with pious acrylic paintings of the siege by modern
                                    artists,
the room with photographs of the march-past of 1931,
and the one gallery with portraits of the Governors of Puebla,
and the other with those of the Presidents of Mexico.

And later too,
where Christians packed the church
on the site where Cortez had sacrificed Aztecs
on their own altars –

Christians in sweatpants,
Christians rocking up in flexitime,
Christians leaping hotfoot from racing bicycles in long tight
                                    black shorts,
Christians carrying 40-watt Puerto Rican briefcases . . .

The sun shone all that day as it did most days,
the young Mexicans were visibly fond of one another,
and red spiky chrysanthemum blossoms were starting to
                                    appear
on the otherwise bare *colorin* trees.

# Diptych

## I

Brueghel might have invented this botched country —
who left room for earthquakes at the back of his landscapes —
paint crusts fissuring up between tectonic plates . . .
Improbable dabs of pines cling to the inclines.

When a farmer falls on his field, he breaks a leg.
When a car ploughs a corner, it leaves a cross with the names.
Cities sprawl for ever on the seismic flats:
food, shanties, transport, *Hispanoquimica* . . .

Trees are cleared for maize, maize is blown to chalk dust.
A national holiday commemorates the ten good years to 1954.
White child coffins are stacked like wedding cake.
A man climbs into his marimba and dies.

II

Icarus was born in Oakland,
but he carried the blue Salvadorean passport
with a dirty thumbprint and his clean-shaven photograph.
He'd been a G-man, then a guerrilla, he had the boots for
                                          either,

had spent some time in Managua, but was no Communist.
He smelled as though he'd been drinking – his own urine, that
                                          is –
and he spoke American English as though he'd heard its
last words, or it was something he'd been paid in . . .

For now, he cruised the fairground with his story,
slept rough, and headed north. He was a passive man,
for all his three stripes, and his air of having got through
several lives, his own included, rather too fast.

## Aerogrammes, 1–5

It felt like my life talking to me – after two months,
talking to me again – saying it had bought a new duvet
but was still dithering on the matter of children,
that it had been seeing a lot of its friends – it wondered
whether it was truly in love with me – and had enjoyed
some pleasantly successful moments at work, but it wasn't
eating or sleeping properly, and was talking far too much.

# Guanajuato Two Times

*for Karl Miller*


I could keep returning to the same few places
till I turned blue; till I turned into
José José
on the sleeve of his new record album,
'What is Love?';
wearing a pleasant frown and predistressed denims;
reading the double-page spread ('The Trouble with José José')
on his drink problem,
comparing his picture 'Before' and 'After' . . .
I could slowly become a ghost, slowly familiar,
slowly invisible, amiable, obtuse . . .
I could say 'Remember me?' to the blank bellhop,
and myself remember
the septet in the bandstand playing 'Winchester Cathedral',
and the clown coming in for coffee
and to count his takings and take off his face . . .
I could take on all my former beds for size.
Meander knowingly through twelve towns with twelve street
                                        names between them.
Sit on both sides of the municipal kissing seats,
shaking my head at the blanket men
and the hammock men, in their humorous desperation
offering me hammocks for four, for five, for six . . .
I could learn the Spanish for
'I shall have returned' or 'Hullo, it's me again!'
and get the hang of the double handshake,
first the palms, then the locked thumbs.
My dreams would moulder and swell and hang off me

like pawpaws. I could stand and sway like a palm,
or rooted like a campanile, crumbling slightly
each time the bells tolled, not real bells
but recordings of former bells,
and never for me.